DOWN in the HAM

a child's guide to downtown birmingham

Ashley Chesnut

illustrated by **Abby Little**

Down in the Ham: A Child's Guide to Downtown Birmingham

To the true God of this city –
our Lord and Savior Jesus Christ.
May You get all of the glory from this endeavor.

✗ · ✗ · ✗ · ✗ · ✗ · ✗ · ✗ · ✗ · ✗

And to the children of Birmingham,
may this book stir in you a greater love for
our city, and may you learn from its
history and make it a better place for us all.

I have a great view of my city, you know,
Standing above and looking below.
But even before I came here to stand,
People were already mining this land.

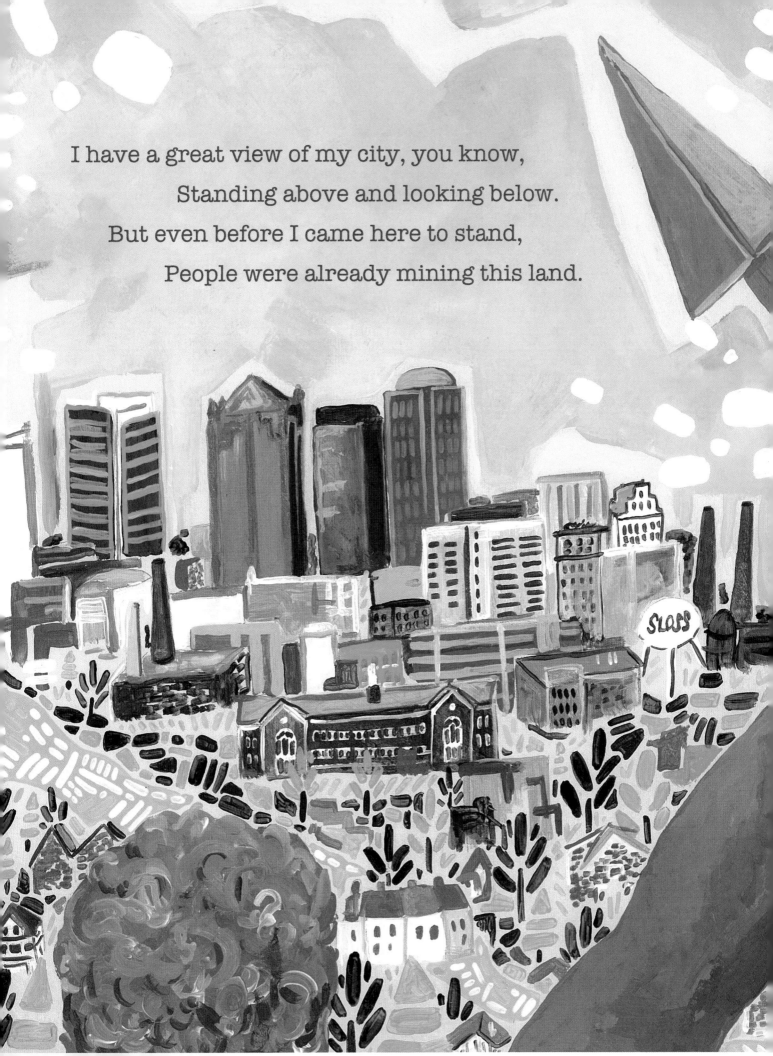

Iron ore and coal –
Of that Birmingham had plenty,
Enough that she would not
Soon run empty.

Furnaces were founded
To make and mold steel
Which the Louisville & Nashville Railroad
Carried across the
land with great zeal.

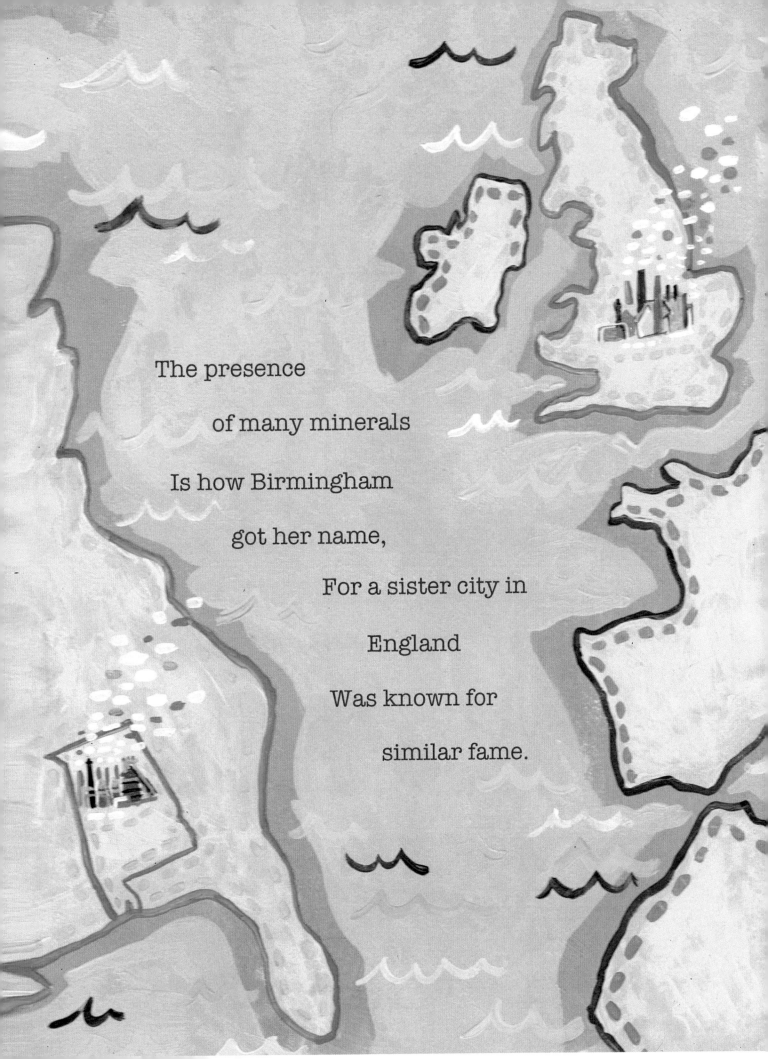

The presence

of many minerals

Is how Birmingham

got her name,

For a sister city in

England

Was known for

similar fame.

Birmingham was
founded in 1871
And grew so quickly
That the "Magic City"
She became known.

But she's had her challenges
From the beginning.
Her history is muddied
And includes some sinning.

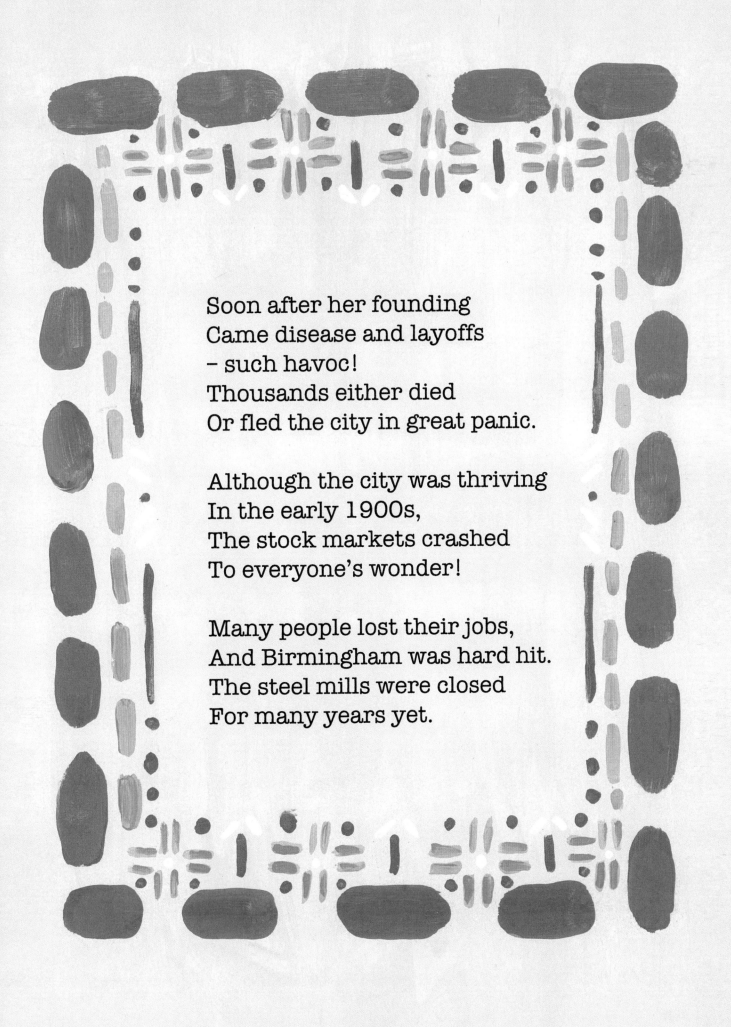

Soon after her founding
Came disease and layoffs
– such havoc!
Thousands either died
Or fled the city in great panic.

Although the city was thriving
In the early 1900s,
The stock markets crashed
To everyone's wonder!

Many people lost their jobs,
And Birmingham was hard hit.
The steel mills were closed
For many years yet.

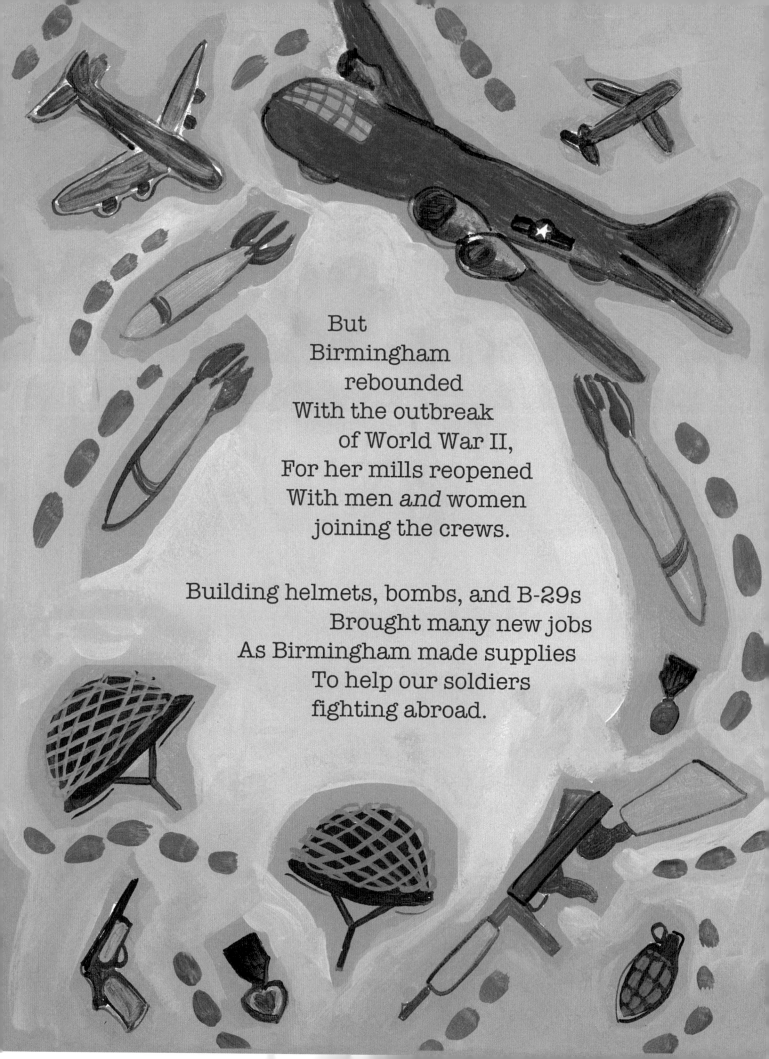

But
Birmingham
rebounded
With the outbreak
of World War II,
For her mills reopened
With men *and* women
joining the crews.

Building helmets, bombs, and B-29s
Brought many new jobs
As Birmingham made supplies
To help our soldiers
fighting abroad.

With many new industries
Launching after the war,
Birmingham again
Had the potential to soar.

But in the 1960s,
Challenges came -
Not from money or illness -
But from not seeing people the same.

I saw Birmingham divided
Between whites and blacks.
White people even fled downtown
Because of the fact.

But the difference of skin color
Is no reason to hate,
So let's learn from our history,
Lest we repeat the same fate.

The hate grew in our city
To such a degree
That a black church downtown
Was bombed in 1963.

Four little girls died
After Sunday School that day.
As you can see,
Birmingham was not okay.

In 1979,
The city voted,
And to the position of mayor
The first *black* man got promoted.

A street downtown
Commemorates this Birmingham son
Who went by the name
Of Richard Arrington.

This street begins
Right in front of me,
And if you follow it closely,
Many sights you will see:

FIVE POINTS SOUTH

Like *The Storyteller* fountain
In Five Points South
Where frogs sit on lily pads
With water shooting from their mouths.

How many woodland creatures are there
Hearing the bronzed ram reading a story?
You'll have to go count them
And take an inventory.

One block from the fountain,
A castle emerges.
Its name is Quinlan,
And its future is uncertain.

Although knights and dragons
This castle lacked all and any,
(It once contained apartments
And provided housing for many.)

But still it was built
With turreted tops.
Look 'round till you see
A cannon ready to pop!

To the left of Richard Arrington,
The home of the Blazers you will see.
Do you know what university this is?
Maybe you'll go there for your degree!

Two downtown treasures
That can never be recovered
Are the Terminal Station and city sign,
Which outside the station used to hover.

But to remember
this iconic piece of history
That has been lost
Is a new sign and a trail
That will connect Railroad Park to Sloss.

Walk the trail with your squad
From beginning to end;
Take a selfie in front of the sign
With all of your friends.

"It's nice to have you in Birmingham"
Will soon greet you on your way,
And if you step inside the diner,
Order the chicken and waffles today!

Two of the oldest
Church buildings in town
Are three blocks apart
And both colored brown.

One has twin spires,
The other a tall tower.
But both are places to go
To worship the God of great
power.

One other church
That had an early beginning
Is known today
As Third Presbyterian.

Its first pastor served the homeless
And the poor for fifty years,
And even after his death,
Others continue that work here.

The hurts of the needy and downtrodden
He did bear,
And when you find his statue in 5 Points,
He will be on his knees in prayer.

A few other sites
That need to be mentioned
(At least while I still have
A bit of your attention):

Include the Civil Rights Institute
And Kelly Ingram Park;
Sadly, the events that occurred there
Are really quite dark.

There you can follow
The Civil Rights Heritage Trail
And learn more of the city's history
Like MLK's "Letter from Birmingham Jail."

Choose one of the trail routes
To discover more of the story,
But I warn you –
Our history is more guts than glory.

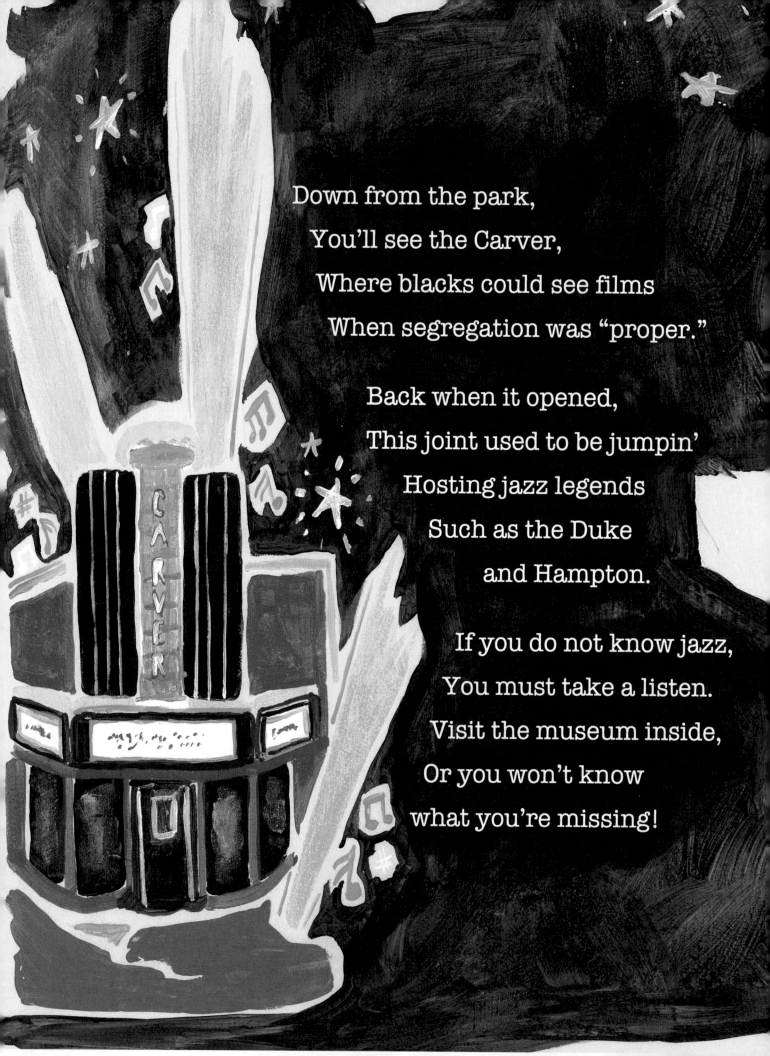

Down from the park,
You'll see the Carver,
Where blacks could see films
When segregation was "proper."

Back when it opened,
This joint used to be jumpin'
Hosting jazz legends
Such as the Duke
and Hampton.

If you do not know jazz,
You must take a listen.
Visit the museum inside,
Or you won't know
what you're missing!

This isn't the only theater
Where you can catch a concert or show;
Just visit the Alabama or Lyric
Down on theater row.

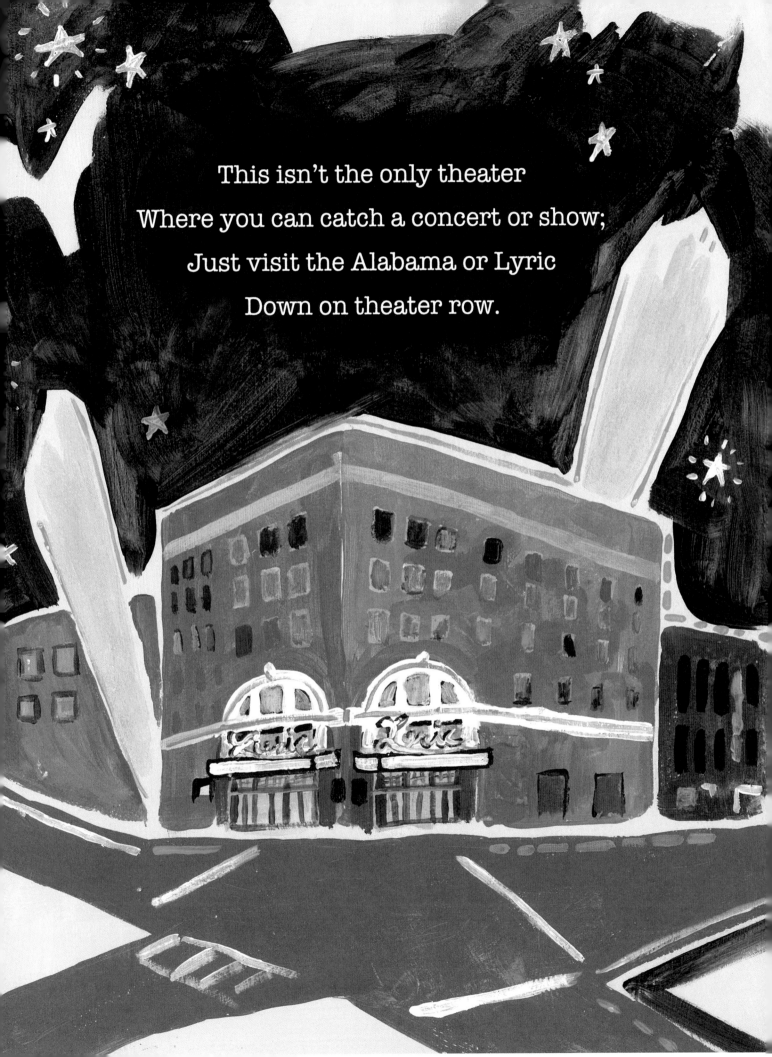

In front of the Alabama,
Follow our state's Walk of Fame.
Do you know
the identities
Of these nineteen
starred names?

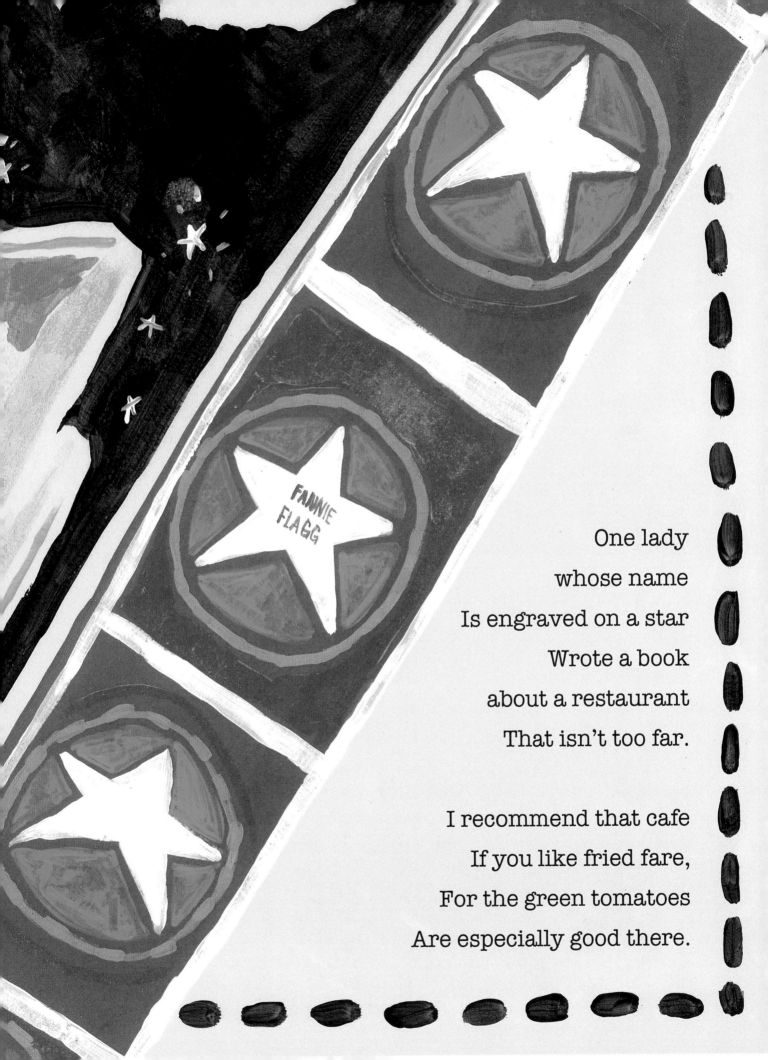

One lady
whose name
Is engraved on a star
Wrote a book
about a restaurant
That isn't too far.

I recommend that cafe
If you like fried fare,
For the green tomatoes
Are especially good there.

One Birmingham tradition
That's been around for ages
Is the Barons playing
On their diamond stages.

However, Regions Field has
Not always been their home.
To see Rickwood Field,
To 2nd Avenue West you must roam.

Birmingham used to have two teams
Known by this name -
One white and one black,
Though they played the same game.

Why are we the Barons?
Have you ever wondered?
I'll give you a clue
That it has to do
With the wealthy mining
and furnace owners.

Next door to the Barons
Is a lovely green space;
Named for the railroads,
It's an ideal exercise and picnic place.

Under the tracks
On two sides of the park
Are Art Deco rainbow tunnels,
Which you should see when it's dark!

So many other places
That I lack time to discuss
Like McWane and Pepper Place -
You'll go there, I trust!

There's also the 9-11 Memorial, Sloss Furnace,
The Pizitz, and the Museum of Art.
Visit them you must;
Please take my words to heart!

"How did I get here?"
Might you be asking,
Standing on Red Mountain
And in the sun basking?

Well, in 1904,
At the St. Louis World's Fair,
Birmingham wanted an exhibit
That would showcase her flair.

Like the
statue in New York,
A colossus I am
Except that I stand high
Over the Ham.

To the Romans,
I was the god of the forge,
Crafting metal jewelry and weapons
In a volcanic gorge.

This is why in my left hand
A hammer I'm holding,
And check out the spear on my right
That *I* finished molding.

When you come see me,
Climb my stairs to the top.
Do you see UAB, Sloss, and Quinlan
In the city's backdrop?

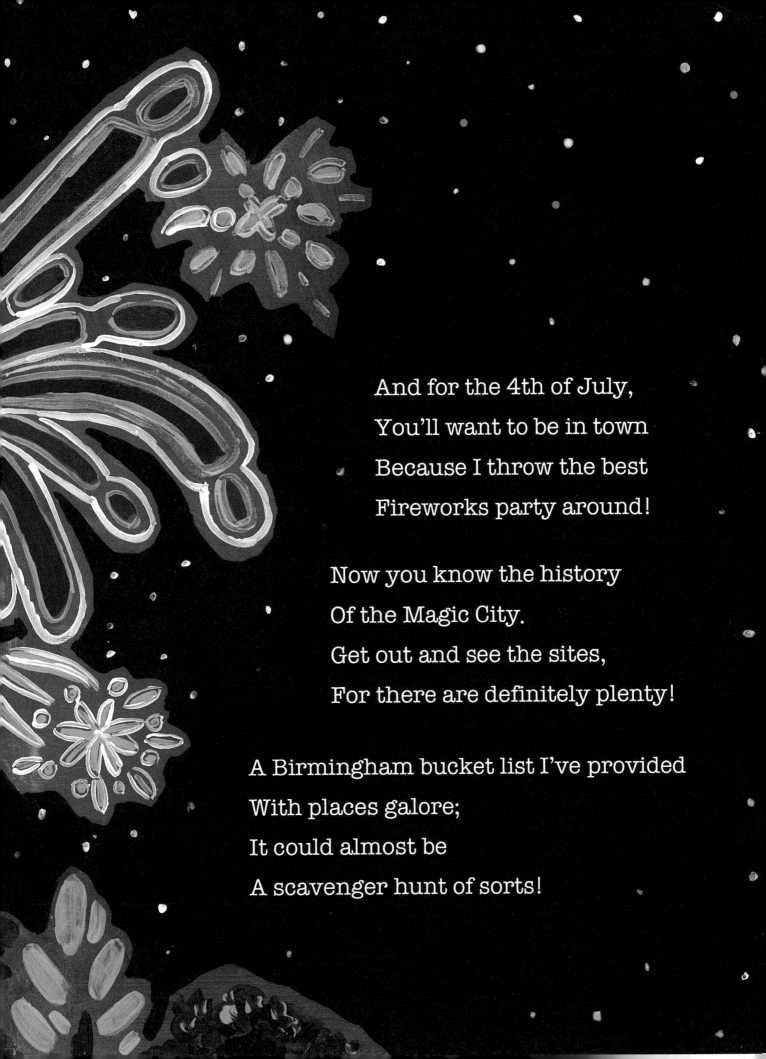

And for the 4th of July,

You'll want to be in town

Because I throw the best

Fireworks party around!

Now you know the history

Of the Magic City.

Get out and see the sites,

For there are definitely plenty!

A Birmingham bucket list I've provided

With places galore;

It could almost be

A scavenger hunt of sorts!

Murals + Signs Map Key

///

1. Vulcan's sign at Vulcan Park & Museum
2. Five Points South inscription on *The Storyteller* fountain
3. Dr. Pepper Co. sign
4. Know Thy Farmer mural
5. Sloss Furnaces' water tower
6. Uptown sign
7. 16th St. Baptist Church sign
8. The Lyric Theatre's sign
9. Vulcan Mural Project
10. Theatre District mural
11. The Alabama Theatre's sign
12. The Birmingham Pledge mural
13. The Pizitz Food Hall sign
14. City Federal Building sign
15. It's Nice to Have You in Birmingham mural
16. Inscription and clock on the John Hand building
17. Rotary Trail in the Magic City sign
18. 1931 sign above the *LightRails*
19. Birmingham Barons' sign at Regions Field
20. Civil Rights Movement mural

For more information about Birmingham's people, places, things, and food, visit
downintheham.com

Made in the USA
Monee, IL
27 February 2021